ROYAL
SHAKESPEARE
COMPANY

RSC School Shakespeare

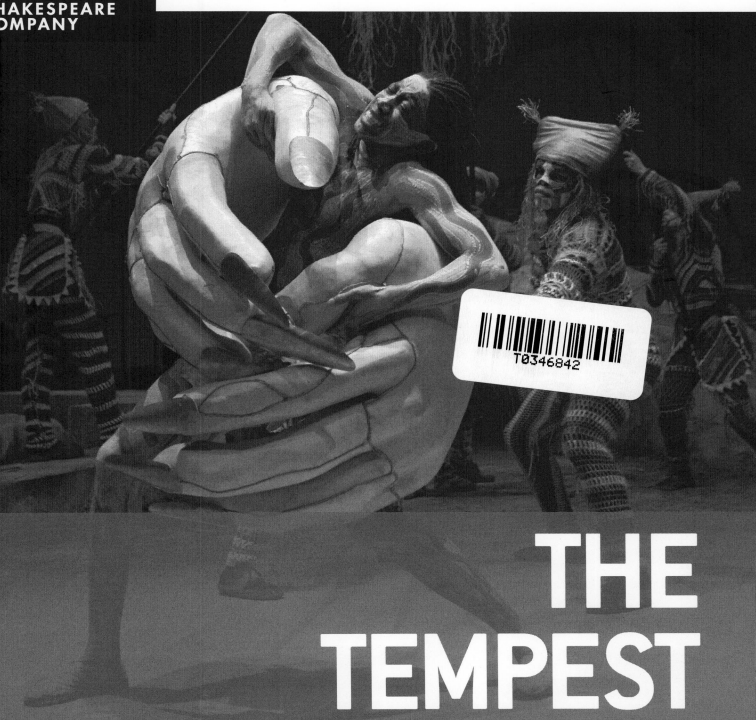

THE TEMPEST

TEACHER GUIDE

OXFORD

UNIVERSITY PRESS

OXFORD
UNIVERSITY PRESS

Great Clarendon Street, Oxford, OX2 6DP, United Kingdom

Oxford University Press is a department of the University of Oxford.

It furthers the University's objective of excellence in research, scholarship, and education by publishing worldwide. Oxford is a registered trade mark of Oxford University Press in the UK and in certain other countries

British Library Cataloguing in Publication Data

Data available

ISBN 978-019-836927-1

10 9 8

Printed and bound by CPI Group (UK) Ltd, Croydon, CR0 4YY

Acknowledgements

We are indebted to all of those teachers and practitioners who have contributed to the development of the work in this series. In particular Cicely Berry whose work is a constant source of inspiration. The material in this guide was primarily written by RSC Head of Professional Development Miles Tandy, with additional input from Rachel Gartside and Tracy Irish. Editorial work for the RSC was undertaken by Jacqui O'Hanlon.

Cover and performance images © Royal Shakespeare Company

Cover image by Ellie Kurttz. Other The Tempest performance images by Manuel Harlan (2006), Ellie Kurttz (2009), Simon Annand (2012) and Topher McGrillis (2016, 2017)

The manufacturer's authorised representative in the EU for product safety is Oxford University Press España S.A. of el Parque Empresarial San Fernando de Henares, Avenida de Castilla, 2 – 28830 Madrid (www.oup.es/en).

Contents

Caliban and the Spirits, *The Tempest*, 2009

Introduction

'You do not understand Shakespeare fully until you have spoken the text aloud. This is because there is something in the physicality of the language which is not only an intrinsic part of the rhythm and form of the writing, but also of the underlying motive and reasoning of the characters involved. And I believe young people of whatever academic ability, given the right opportunity to speak the language, latch on to this in a remarkable way and I know it excites them and makes them want more.'

Cicely Berry, RSC Voice Director

RSC Rehearsal

The classroom as rehearsal room

All the work of RSC Education is underpinned by the artistic practice of the Royal Shakespeare Company (RSC). In particular, we make very strong connections between the rehearsal rooms in which our actors and directors work and the classrooms in which you and your students work. Rehearsal rooms are essentially places of exploration and shared discovery, in which a company of actors and their director work together to bring Shakespeare's plays to life. To do this successfully, they need to have a deep understanding of the text, to get the language 'in the body', to speak it as if it is 'fresh-minted', and to be open to a range of interpretive possibilities and choices. The ways in which they do this are both active and playful, connecting mind, voice and body. They are also approaches that young people take to readily, allowing them to explore complex language confidently and openly.

Becoming a company

To do this we begin by deliberately building a spirit of one group with a shared purpose – this is about *us* rather than *me*. We often do this with games that warm up our brains, voices and bodies, and we continue to build this spirit through a scheme of work by shared, collaborative tasks that depend on and value everyone's contributions. The ways in which we work encourage young people to discuss, speculate and question – there is rarely one right answer. This process requires and develops critical thinking.

Making the world of the play

In rehearsals at the RSC, we explore the whole world of the play: we tackle the language, characters and motivation, setting, plot and themes, but we do that through a collective act of imagination, in which we bring to life the human experiences the play contains. Every member of the company is implicated, contributing their ideas and skills, so they become fully invested. In our rehearsal-based classrooms, a similar investment can take place. By 'standing in the shoes' of the characters and inhabiting the world of the play, students are implicated and engaged with their whole selves: head, eyes, ears, hands, bodies and hearts are involved in actively interpreting the play. In grappling with scenes and speeches, students are also actively grappling with the themes and ideas in the play, experiencing them from the point of view of the characters. Students should have the opportunity to identify themes as they arise from exploring the action, and make their understanding of those themes specific by relating them to their experiences of the world of the play.

The text is central to our discoveries

At the heart of this pedagogy is the idea of young people encountering Shakespeare as fellow artists. Working with his language in the same ways that actors do, they can create outcomes that offer real insight into the text, in which they can take great pride and which are often genuinely beautiful. For the actor in the rehearsal room, there is little distinction between play and work; they make plays for a living. The playful approaches we ask students to commit to and take seriously are real work in the real world.

We place the text at the core of everything we do. Whatever the abilities of the young people you teach, active, playful approaches can make Shakespeare's language vivid, accessible and enjoyable. His words have the power to excite and delight all of us.

Pushing back the desks

In the rehearsal room, the RSC uses social and historical contexts in order to deepen understanding of the world of the play. The company is engaged in a 'conversation across time', inviting audiences to consider what a play means to us now and what it meant to us then. We hope that the activities in this resource will offer your students an opportunity to join that conversation.

You will not need any specialist training in the fields of Shakespeare or drama to teach using this resource. All of the activities can be done in a normal English classroom, although occasionally you might push back the desks. The pedagogy you will find in these pages has been developed with teachers who work in a wide variety of classroom settings with students of all abilities and backgrounds. The activities require close, critical reading and encourage students to make informed interpretive choices about language, character and motivation, themes and plot. Often, the activities invite an intuitive, spontaneous response which is developed through questioning. The work is rooted in speaking and listening to Shakespeare's words and to each other's ideas. This way of working can produce sophisticated analytical responses, both oral and written, challenging the most able learners as well as motivating the most reluctant.

Building a classroom culture that values and celebrates this pedagogy takes time. For many young people, it may make demands on them that are unfamiliar, even uncomfortable to begin with. But persist and the rewards can be great, as students grow in confidence, embracing and unlocking this extraordinary literary inheritance.

Using *RSC School Shakespeare*

This resource will support you to teach Shakespeare using the pedagogy of the RSC rehearsal room. As you open each spread, you will see the complete script of the play on the right hand page. Accompanying the script, on the left hand page, are a series of features which we hope will enable you to work actively in your classroom. Those features are:

Summary

At the top of every page is a summary of what happens on the facing page. This is provided so that students can efficiently and easily contextualise the text and understand the action.

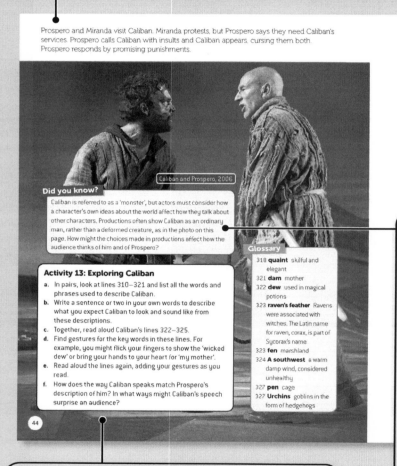

Prospero and Miranda visit Caliban. Miranda protests, but Prospero says they need Caliban's services. Prospero calls Caliban with insults and Caliban appears, cursing them both. Prospero responds by promising punishments.

Act 1 | Scene 2

Prospero	Shake it off. Come on. We'll visit Caliban, my slave, who never Yields us kind answer.
Miranda	'Tis a villain, sir, I do not love to look on.

Caliban and Prospero, 2006

Did you know?
Caliban is referred to as a 'monster', but actors must consider how a character's own ideas about the world affect how they talk about other characters. Productions often show Caliban as an ordinary man, rather than a deformed creature, as in the photo on this page. How might the choices made in productions affect how the audience thinks of him and of Prospero?

Glossary
318 **quaint** skilful and elegant
321 **dam** mother
322 **dew** used in magical potions
323 **raven's feather** Ravens were associated with witches. The Latin name for raven, corax, is part of Sycorax's name
323 **fen** marshland
324 **A southwest** a warm damp wind, considered unhealthy
327 **pen** cage
327 **Urchins** goblins in the form of hedgehogs

Activity 13: Exploring Caliban
a. In pairs, look at lines 310–321 and list all the words and phrases used to describe Caliban.
b. Write a sentence or two in your own words to describe what you expect Caliban to look and sound like from these descriptions.
c. Together, read aloud Caliban's lines 322–325.
d. Find gestures for the key words in these lines. For example, you might flick your fingers to show the 'wicked dew' or bring your hands to your heart for 'my mother'.
e. Read aloud the lines again, adding your gestures as you read.
f. How does the way Caliban speaks match Prospero's description of him? In what ways might Caliban's speech surprise an audience?

44

RSC production photographs

Every page includes at least one photograph from an RSC production of the play. Some of the activities make direct use of the production photographs. The photographs illustrate the action, bringing to life the text on the page. They also include a caption that identifies the characters or event, together with the date of the RSC production.

Did you know?

For every scene, we have provided insight into RSC rehearsal practice, so that students can link the work they are doing in the classroom to the work that is done by actors, directors and designers at the RSC. We hope that students will see themselves as fellow artists, working alongside the professionals, exploring the play in a similar way.

For your teaching needs, you may choose to work on key scenes. However, if you work through the whole play from beginning to end, using the activities on each page, you will be taking your students on a progressive learning journey. Their journey parallels the journey which the RSC follows in rehearsal for a production: a collaborative, cumulative exploration. Some activities may feel more comfortable for your teaching style or environment than others, and you may, of course, choose to use the activities alongside your own classroom approaches.

Activity
Every page includes at least one classroom activity which is inspired by RSC rehearsal room practice.

Glossary
Where needed, there is a glossary which explains those words which may be unfamiliar to students and cannot be worked out in context.

Miranda is distressed at watching a ship wrecked offshore and believes her father Prospero has created the storm using his magical powers. Prospero assures her that no one on the ship has been harmed. He announces that it is time for her to know more about their past.

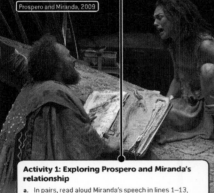

Prospero and Miranda, 2009

Glossary
1 **your art** skills of magic
2 **allay** calm
3 **pitch** a thick black substance like tar
4 **welkin's** sky's
5 **fire** lightning
6 **brave vessel** impressive ship
13 **fraughting souls** the people who form the ship's freight
20 **cell** a small, simple home

Activity 1: Exploring Prospero and Miranda's relationship
a. In pairs, read aloud Miranda's speech in lines 1–13, swapping reader at each punctuation mark.
b. Discuss how you think Miranda feels as she speaks. Which words suggest this?
c. The stage direction simply says 'Enter Prospero and Miranda'. Discuss what the audience might see before Miranda speaks. Do they enter together? Do we see Prospero first, conducting the storm? Or Miranda first, watching the storm?
d. With one of you playing Miranda and the other playing Prospero, create a **freeze-frame** of the moment before Miranda speaks.
e. Now look at lines 16–17 and create a second freeze-frame showing this moment.
f. Share your freeze-frames and discuss what we can **infer** about Prospero and Miranda from these two moments.

At the time
Using page 191, find out more about beliefs in witches and sorcery in Shakespeare's time. What do you think audiences in Shakespeare's time and our own might think about Prospero's ability to create storms?

Key terms
Freeze-frame a physical, still image created by people to represent an object, place, person or feeling
Infer form an opinion based on evidence

22

Act 1 | Scene 2

Enter Prospero and Miranda

Miranda	If by your art, my dearest father, you have	
	Put the wild waters in this roar, allay them.	
	The sky, it seems, would pour down stinking pitch,	
	But that the sea, mounting to the welkin's cheek,	
	Dashes the fire out. O, I have suffered	5
	With those that I saw suffer! A brave vessel,	
	Who had, no doubt, some noble creature in her,	
	Dashed all to pieces. O, the cry did knock	
	Against my very heart! Poor souls, they perished.	
	Had I been any god of power, I would	10
	Have sunk the sea within the earth or ere	
	It should the good ship so have swallowed, and	
	The fraughting souls within her.	
Prospero	Be collected.	
	No more amazement. Tell your piteous heart	
	There's no harm done.	
Miranda	O, woe the day!	
Prospero	No harm.	15
	I have done nothing but in care of thee,	
	Of thee, my dear one, thee, my daughter, who	
	Art ignorant of what thou art, nought knowing	
	Of whence I am, nor that I am more better	
	Than Prospero, master of a full poor cell,	20
	And thy no greater father.	
Miranda	More to know	
	Did never meddle with my thoughts.	
Prospero	'Tis time	
	I should inform thee farther. Lend thy hand	

23

Key terms
Where needed, there is an explanation of any key terms used, literary or theatrical.

At the time
There are simple social and historical research tasks, so that students can use knowledge from the time the play was written to help them interpret the script. The social and historical information can be found towards the back of the edition of the play.

Editing choices

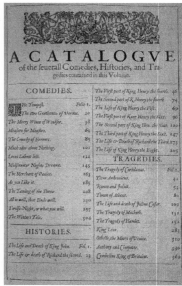

A list of the plays contained in the First Folio of William Shakespeare 1623

Following his death in 1616, two of Shakespeare's friends and colleagues, John Heminges and Henry Condell, put together a collection of his plays which was published in 1623, known as the First Folio, and this edition of the play is based on the First Folio text.

Punctuation

Our text has been edited for punctuation, and choices based on clarity have been made where wording and lineation vary between Folio and Quarto★. Fashions in punctuation change but its purpose is always to support the reader's understanding. In this edition, our motive has been to keep the punctuation as simple and clear as possible but to avoid influencing students' choices. Exclamation marks, for example, are rarely used in the First Folio whereas today's fashion is to use them more liberally. In this edition, they have been used only when they appear in the First Folio or when it is clear an exclamation is required, such as calling out a greeting. In most cases, sentences end in full stops, allowing the students to decide the tone of a line and whether they feel it should be spoken as an exclamation, a statement or a question.

Stage directions

Similarly, there are very few stage directions in the First Folio but those that do exist most probably reflect the stage business as originally performed. Where these stage directions do exist, we have kept them so that students can choose to follow them or not. Generally, Shakespeare gives us important stage directions in the text; for example entrances are often marked by 'Here comes…'. Students are encouraged in the activities to discover directions for action written in the text and to add their own choices about actions and movements appropriate for the scene.

★ The Quarto was a smaller format of publication. As with the larger Folio editions, many versions of the Quarto were produced with variations in editorial decisions

Prospero and Miranda, *The Tempest*, 2009

Working collaboratively

When a new group of actors and their director come together to rehearse at the RSC, time is spent on the practical, playful process of building a company. This is partly achieved by 'warming up' through a series of physical and vocal games and exercises, before exploring together whichever scenes and speeches are in the rehearsal schedule for that day.

Starter activities

In the classroom, the equivalent to the 'warm up' would be the 'starter' activity, which scaffolds the main activity of the lesson. In a rehearsal-based classroom, starter activities should build physical and vocal confidence, communication skills and positive relationships, as well as introducing any new knowledge required for the lesson. For example, if you are going to ask your students to work in pairs to explore a dialogue, you might start the lesson with a game. If the dialogue you are going to be exploring is full of conflict, the game you choose might be one in which your students can score points against their partner. Or, if you want the focus to be on the quality of the relationship between the two characters, you might ask pairs to make a freeze-frame which shows their initial interpretation of that relationship, before going on to explore the dialogue in more detail.

Grouping

We have left grouping as open as possible, so that you can use the activities flexibly. While some of them can be done as individuals, we recommend that you enable your students to collaborate wherever possible. Interpretation in rehearsal always comes from sharing and valuing each other's ideas, questioning assumptions and speculating possibilities, which we can only do with others. Often the number of characters in a scene will lead naturally to grouping in your classroom. If a scene has four characters, a group of four should explore it. If you don't have the right number of students to make equal sized groups, there is a benefit in having an 'extra' group member who can either bring in another point of view as a non-speaking character (for example, as a servant in a court scene) or fulfil a directorial function, acting as an outside eye for the rest of their group as they decide how to interpret a scene together.

Examples of flexible grouping activities include:
- Activity 1, page 62
- Activity 7, page 74
- Activity 2, page 120

Spirits, Ferdinand and Ariel, *The Tempest*, 2009

Questioning

Good questioning is crucial both in encouraging students to experiment with ideas and in leading their reflections after each activity. Students will often have found an embodied understanding through the activities, but without time spent articulating that understanding it can easily dissipate.

Using open questions

Open questions are often defined as questions to which you cannot respond with one 'right' answer or with a simple yes or no. The questions we offer in these activities are framed to avoid yes/no answers and encourage students to reflect more deeply on the understanding they have gained actively. These questions are far from exhaustive and we would urge you to ask others.

Making personal connections

One successful approach is to ask questions that encourage students to link the emotions and situations of the play with emotions and situations they can relate to from their own experiences and imaginations. Opening questions you can always ask are:

- How did that exercise make you feel?
- What discoveries did you make by speaking the text in that way?

Some students need more time to think and process their thoughts than others. Paired or group reflections are very useful in giving each student more opportunity to express and develop their responses in dialogue with each other. This can be followed by a whole class plenary in which more students can be encouraged to take part because they have had time to formulate their ideas.

Many teachers have found that asking students to record their thoughts and ideas in journals as they work through their study of the play is hugely beneficial and provides personalised notes to return to when completing assessments.

> **Open questions appear on every page but examples of activities with more open questions include:**
> - Activity 2, page 18
> - Activity 1, page 22
> - Activity 8, page 166

Antonio and Sebastian, *The Tempest*, 2016

Creating a character

Character motivation

In order for an actor to play a character, they must first understand what motivates their character. The questions that actors and their director ask about the characters in a scene are often deceptively simple: 'Who are they?', 'In what time period and time of day is the scene taking place?', 'Where are they?', 'What are they doing?', 'What are they trying to achieve?', 'Why are they doing that?' It is through these basic questions that the company begin to bring the play to life. By asking these questions of themselves and each other, the company have to search for clues in the text which help them to decide what is motivating the characters.

Developing the 'given circumstances'

Actors pay attention to the 'given circumstances' of a scene, or those things that we know from the text. For example, in asking 'Where are they?', the company might know from the text that a scene is set in 'a room in the castle', but which room? What are the values, social customs and atmosphere of the place? In asking 'Who are they?', the company might know that the characters are father and daughter, but they must work out what the exact nature of the relationship is and how it evolves, the shifting status of the characters, their 'backstory' (or what has happened between them before the play starts), and what has happened in the play thus far to affect the characters and their actions. Character motivation is discovered by actively exploring the evidence in the text to make informed interpretations.

The activities in this resource are designed to help students answer the basic questions about character for themselves: Who? What? Where? When? Why? so that they can work out character motivation. A company of actors rehearsing a play at the RSC ask each other questions all the time, and we recommend that you encourage students to ask each other these questions as they work. Using the activities will offer your students plenty of opportunities to do just that.

> **Examples of activities requiring students to ask questions about characters include:**
> - Activity 4, page 28
> - Activity 13, page 44
> - Activity 17, page 52

Caliban and Stephano, *The Tempest*, 2016

Layering

In rehearsal, actors and their director explore the same part of the text in different ways, with the aim of developing a deep understanding of that part of the action. It is a cumulative, layered process, in which multiple possibilities for interpretation are explored. Then, the company make mutually agreed, informed interpretive choices based on the evidence in the text.

Extending learning opportunities

In order to emulate this rehearsal process in the classroom, we recommend offering a series of short activities, which build on each other but explore a different aspect of the text each time. This can enable close reading and active engagement, but avoid students getting bored working on the same part of the text. In this resource, we have usually offered a single activity for exploring the text on each page, for the sake of clarity. But, as you work through the activities with your class, you will notice strategies which could easily be transferred to use with a different part of the text. If there is a particular scene which you want your students to focus on more fully, we hope you will consider transferring some of the activities from other pages to enable a deeper understanding of your focus scene. In this way, we can layer and extend the learning opportunities for our students.

> **Examples of activities which use several strategies to layer understanding in this way include:**
> - Activity 2, page 110
> - Activity 3, page 112
> - Activity 5, page 116

Repeating activities

In the rehearsal room, it is common practice for the company to explore each new scene or speech in a play using familiar activities. A shared set of approaches is deliberately developed. Because the strategies are applied to different parts of the text, they feel fresh each time. Similarly, in the rehearsal-based classroom, we deliberately apply the same strategies to different parts of the text so that our students have the opportunity to become familiar and more confident with those activities. In so doing, we build layers of understanding and engagement. As you explore this resource, you will notice strategies that are repeated. We hope you will also notice how the same activities can produce widely differentiated outcomes, simply because they are applied to a different part of the text.

> **Examples of activities highlighting structure include:**
> - Activity 13, page 84
> - Activity 1, page 86
> - Activity 7, page 96

One of the outcomes of using this layered approach can be to highlight the structure of a play. In the many plays where Shakespeare offers a parallel or 'sub' plot alongside the main action, using the same active strategies to explore parallel events in the play can enable our students to see the similarities (and differences) between them.

Ferdinand and Miranda, *The Tempest,* 2016

Creative constraints

In order to test the relationships between characters in an RSC rehearsal room, actors often find it useful to try exercises that put some kind of limitation on how they respond. By applying this limitation, actors make discoveries about what the lines could mean and about their relationship with other characters. Using the same exercises, students can experiment with different ways to interpret a scene and can discuss what feels right for them in expressing the relationship between their characters and why.

Movement choices

In some activities students are asked to choose between simple movements. Giving students simple but specific choices to make removes the fear of 'acting' but also means they can't just stand still and speak because standing still becomes a choice, not a default. In making these simple choices, students find intuitive responses led by the words their own character speaks or the words that are spoken to them. These exercises are also useful for thinking about characters present in a scene who have no, or few, lines. These characters are still required to make the choices about movement and other characters have to respond to what they do.

Examples of activities exploring movement include:
- Activity 7, page 34
- Activity 18, page 54
- Activity 8, page 76

Speaking choices

In other activities, students are given constraints about how they speak. For example, they can compare how whispering lines and then speaking them loudly brings out different qualities of expression; how reading aloud and swapping reader on each punctuation mark can clarify sense but also express whether a character is feeling calm or agitated; how speaking to achieve a simple objective, like getting another character to look at you, brings language alive by giving a character a reason to speak.

Examples of activities exploring speaking choices include:
- Activity 12, page 82
- Activity 1, page 100
- Activity 3, page 122

Stephano, Ariel and Caliban, *The Tempest*, 2006

Speaking text aloud

Unlike many of the other texts we tackle with our students, a play text is intended to be shared aloud, between characters on stage and with the audience. The text is not simply black marks on a piece of paper, but words that are meant to be expressed and received orally and aurally. In the RSC rehearsal room, the company of actors and their director use the text as a script, to be shared. One of the challenges of working with a play which is four hundred years old is that it has been done many times before. Nevertheless, each new company which tackles the play will go through the process of speaking and listening to the words, negotiating meaning until a unique, new version of the play is discovered. We can offer the same opportunity to our students, in a speaking and listening process which can lead to highly engaged and personalised responses to the text.

Making meaning

Examples of activities making meaning include:
- Activity 10, page 38
- Activity 5, page 126
- Activity 2, page 132

A word on the page may appear to have a fixed meaning, but when that word is spoken, the meaning of the word is dependent on the intention of the speaker. Consider for a moment the word 'yes'. We all know the dictionary definition of that word. However, when the word 'yes' is spoken as if the speaker is doubtful, it means something entirely different than when the same word, 'yes', is spoken as if the speaker is excited. Tone, pitch, volume and pace are essential to the meaning of the spoken word. So, in rehearsal, meaning is negotiated by speaking the text aloud, exploring and experimenting until a consensus is reached. The activities in this resource offer students the opportunity to follow the same process.

Getting the language 'in the body'

Examples of getting the language 'in the body' include:
- Activity 6, page 140
- Activity 2, page 154
- Activity 5, page 160

Actors and directors at the RSC refer to 'getting the language in the body', by which they mean doing exercises which connect them with the sound and rhythm of the words. The phonic and poetic quality of the language is as important as the literal meaning of the words. Sound and rhythm are deeply affective, experienced on an instinctive level. By voicing and hearing the words, actors can experience the effect of the language. We can offer the same opportunity to our students by encouraging them to speak and listen to the words through the activities in this resource.

Embodying text

Embodying the text is an actor's job. A fundamental aspect of exploring the plays as plays is being on your feet, stepping into the shoes of the characters, experiencing what it is like to be Beatrice or Juliet, Shylock or Banquo, and able to express your thoughts and feelings as articulately as they do. Working with play texts provides excellent opportunities for developing every student's inbuilt facility for communication skills. Just as most of us naturally and easily learn to speak as very young children, we naturally and easily learn to read body language. Students with English as an Additional Language (EAL) and less confident readers often thrive with this work because they can use their understanding of gesture and tone.

> **Examples of activities embodying text:**
> - Activity 14, page 46
> - Activity 2, page 120
> - Activity 2, page 132

Freeze-frames

Freeze-frames are frequently suggested in our activities because they can quickly tap into the key themes in the plays or physically summarise a relationship. For example, a freeze-frame of 'a royal leader and his subjects' created by the students themselves enables a kinaesthetic, imaginative understanding of abstract notions like status and hierarchy to deconstruct through questioning. Freeze-frames of 'brothers' or 'father and daughter' can provide a spectrum of attitudes: love, happiness, fear, disappointment, resentment. Acknowledging these different possibilities can provide a quick and easy insight into the complexity of family relationships. Discussion of these images can lead us into the world of the play by making it relevant to our own worlds. Asking students to create a freeze-frame from a line of text, or asking students to adjust a freeze-frame to reflect or include a line of text are ways to deepen connections between our physical, emotional and intellectual understanding of the text.

> **Examples of activities using freeze frames include:**
> - Activity 1, page 22
> - Activity 11, page 40
> - Activity 1, page 118

Gestures

Other activities ask students to find 'gestures' for key words. In a similar way to working with freeze-frames, these activities support an intellectual understanding of the text through physical associations. For example, creating gestures for the rich imagery of the oppositional elements in antithesis can support appreciation of the internal conflicts a character feels.

> **Examples of activities exploring gesture include:**
> - Activity 6, page 32
> - Activity 8, page 36
> - Activity 2, page 64

Rhythm

Working with the rhythms of the text can give an actor important understanding of how a character might be feeling. You will notice that activities ask students to engage physically with rhythm through galloping, clapping or tapping. This physical approach makes it very clear when there are variations or disturbances to the rhythm so that students can consider what the variations might suggest about a character's state of mind, and how Shakespeare crafts his writing around unfolding rhythms.

> **Examples of activities exploring rhythm include:**
> - Activity 2, page 24
> - Activity 3, page 26
> - Activity 2, page 102

Glossary

Adjective a word that describes a noun, e.g. blue, happy, big

Adverb a word that describes a verb, e.g. quickly

Alliteration words that begin with the same sound

Aside when a character addresses a remark to the audience, or to another character, that other characters on the stage do not hear

Atmosphere the mood created by staging choices

Back-story what happened to any of the characters before the start of the play

Casting deciding which actors should play which roles

Clown an actor skilled in comedy and improvisation who could often sing and dance as well

Dialogue a discussion between two or more people

Dramatic irony when the audience knows something that some characters in the play do not

Emphasis stress given to words when speaking

Extended metaphor describing something by comparing it to something else over several lines

Freeze-frame a physical, still image created by people to represent an object, place, person or feeling

Gesture a movement, often using the hands or head, to express a feeling or idea

Iambic pentameter the rhythm Shakespeare uses to write his plays. Each line in this rhythm contains approximately ten syllables. 'Iambic' means putting the stress on the second syllable of each beat. 'Pentameter' means five beats with two syllables in each beat

Imagery visually descriptive language

Improvise make up in the moment

Infer form an opinion based on evidence

Metaphor describing something by comparing it with something else

Monologue a long speech in which a character expresses their thoughts. Other characters may be present

Objective what a character wants to get or achieve in a scene

Pace the speed at which someone speaks

Paraphrase a line or section of text expressed in your own words

Personification giving an object or concept human qualities

Plot the events of a story

Prop an object used in the play, e.g. a dagger

Quatrain a stanza of four lines

Shared lines lines of iambic pentameter shared between characters. This implies a closeness between them in some way

Simile a comparison that uses the words 'like' or 'as'

Soliloquy a speech in which a character is alone on stage and expresses their thoughts and feelings aloud to the audience

Stage direction an instruction in the text of a play, e.g. indicating which characters enter and exit a scene

Staging the process of selecting, adapting and developing the stage space in which a play will be performed

Subplot a minor plot often reflecting themes of the main plot

Syllable part of a word that is one sound, e.g. 'tempest' has two syllables 'tem' and 'pest'

Tactics the methods a character uses to get what they want

Theme the main ideas explored in a piece of literature, e.g. the themes of power and authority, hope and fear, family, vengeance and forgiveness might be considered key themes of The Tempest

Tone as in 'tone of voice'; expressing an attitude through how you say something

Unit of action one moment, or 'beat' of something happening, which can be described in one sentence

Verb a word describing an action or a state, e.g. jump, shout, believe, exist

Vox pop comment or opinion from a member of the public